NATIONAL GEOGRAPHIC

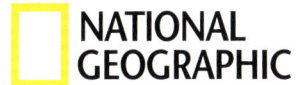

See the U.S.A.

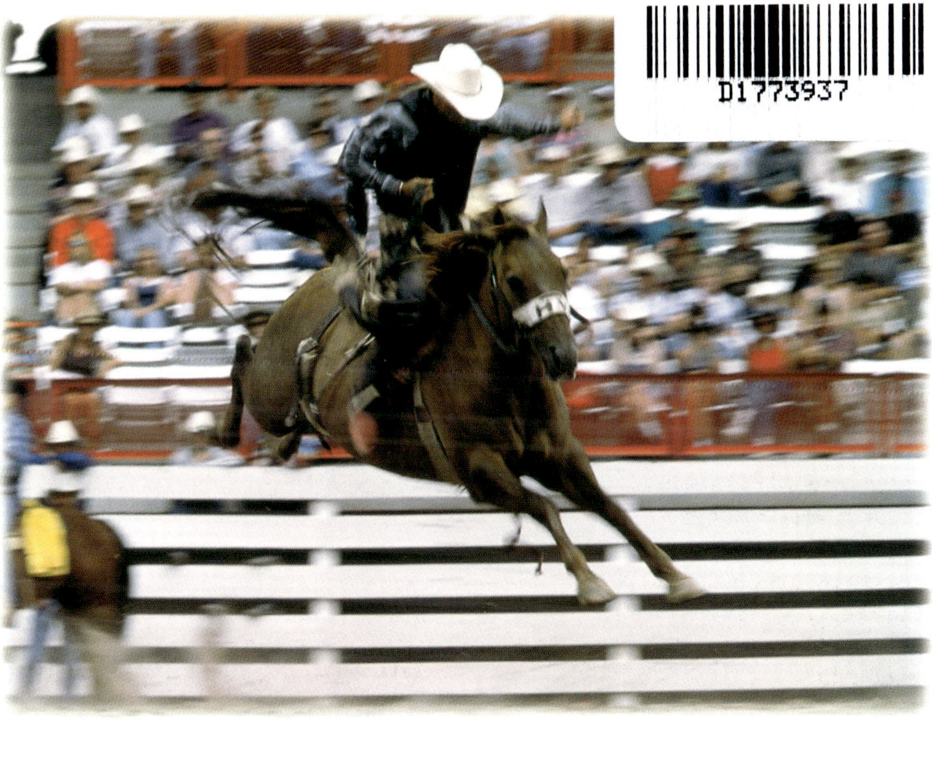

Jaime Schwartz

One Big Country

The United States of America is a big country. It is made up of 50 states. To the east is the Atlantic Ocean. To the west is the Pacific Ocean. To the north is Canada. To the south is Mexico.

As you travel across the country, you will see tall mountains and grassy plains. You will see big cities and wide open spaces.

Five Regions

One way to learn about this huge country is to group the states into regions. The United States can be divided into five regions:

- Northeast
- Southeast
- Midwest
- Southwest
- West

Let's take a look at each region of the United States to see how they are alike and how they are different.

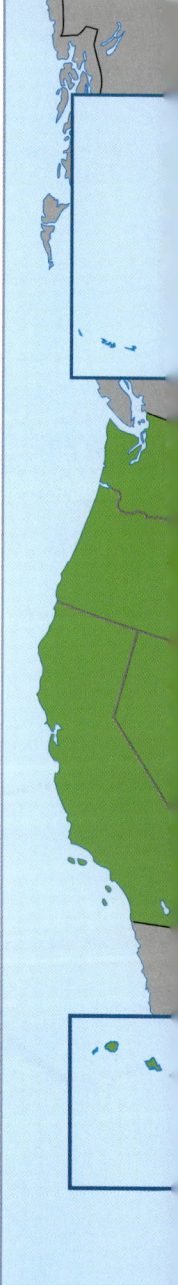

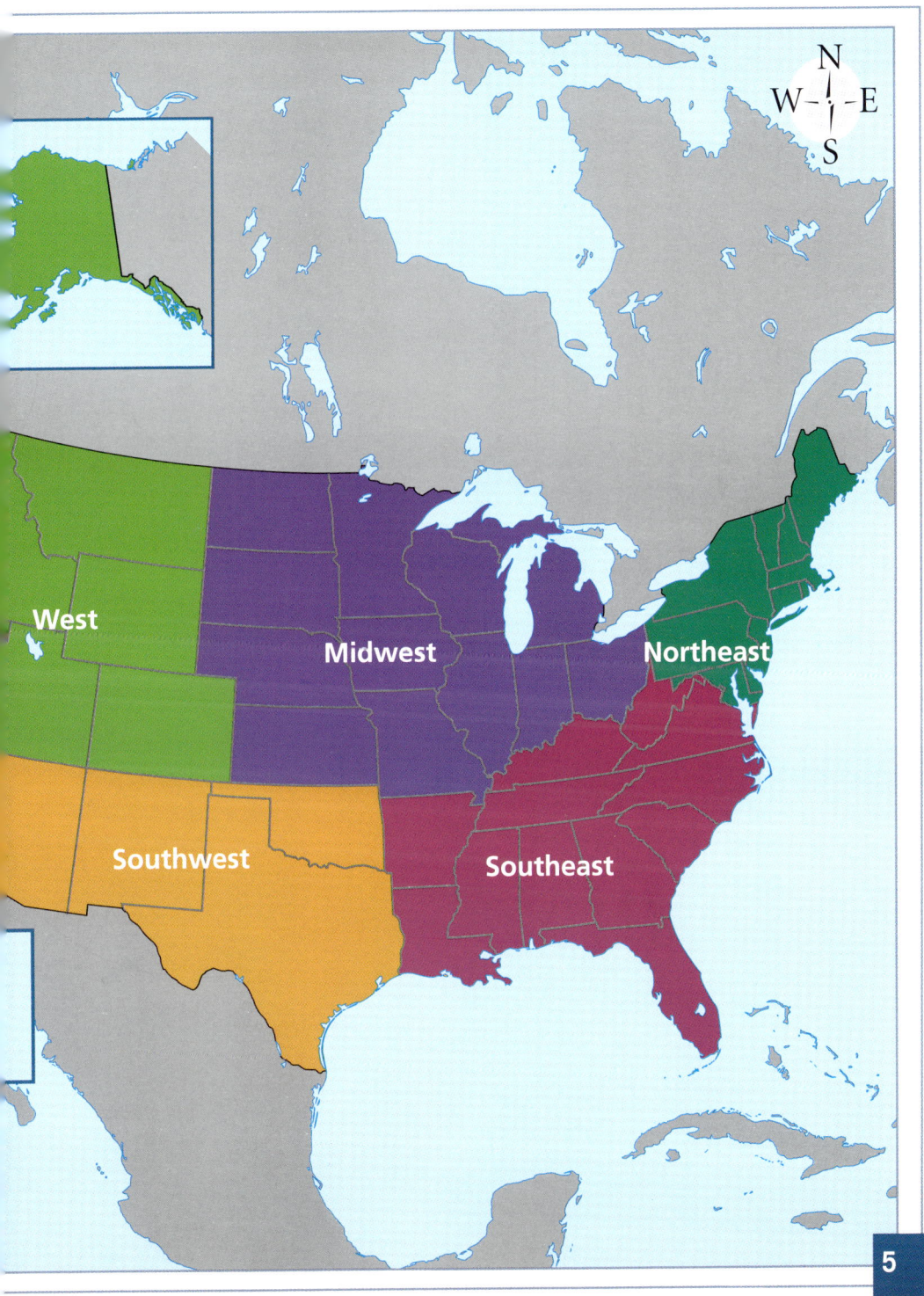

The Northeast Region

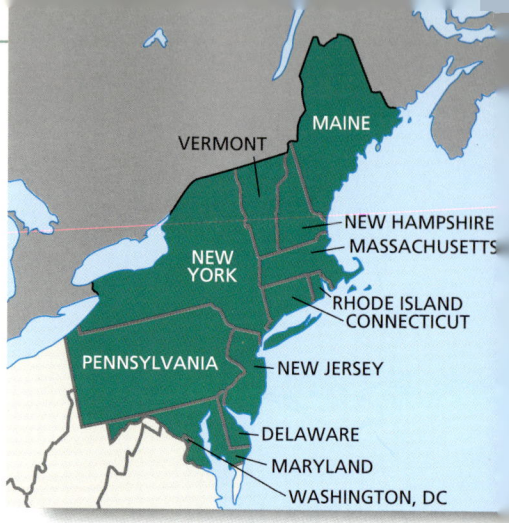

Most of the states in the Northeast are small. One of these states, Rhode Island, is the smallest state in the country. Most of the states border the Atlantic Ocean. Many people live in the Northeast. This region has many large cities.

▼ People enjoy hiking in the Appalachian Mountains.

Seasons bring ▶ change to this region. In the fall, the leaves turn beautiful colors.

▼ Washington, D.C., the capital of the United States, is in this region. The White House is the home of the President.

▲ New York City is the largest city in the United States. Over seven million people live here.

The Southeast Region

The Southeast region has rolling hills and warm wetlands. A wetland is a wet area like a swamp or marsh. The Southeast gets a lot of sunshine. Florida is called the "Sunshine State." Oranges, peanuts, and other crops grow well in the region's warm climate.

▼ Most of the states are along the Atlantic coast. Many people come here to enjoy the ocean.

Swamps and marshes ▶ are home to many plants and animals.

▼ Many fabrics are made in the Southeast. This region is also the number one region for making clothes and furniture.

▲ New Orleans is located on the Mississippi River near the Gulf of Mexico. From New Orleans, goods are shipped all over the world.

The Midwest Region

The Midwest is the flattest region in the United States. This region has very cold winters and very hot summers. This region is known for its many farms. Today, the Midwest produces most of the country's corn and wheat.

▼ Dairy farms in the Midwest produce milk, butter, and cheese.

The biggest city in the region is ▶ Chicago, Illinois. The Sears Tower, one of many skyscrapers in the city, is the tallest building in the U.S.

◀ Cars and trucks are made in factories in the Midwest.

The Great Lakes is the ▶ largest body of fresh water in the world. This ship is carrying iron across the Great Lakes.

The Southwest Region

The Southwest region is the driest and the sunniest region. Here you will see desert lands where tall cacti grow. You will also see wide open spaces where cattle graze and people drill for oil.

▼ Desert plants survive by storing water in their trunks.

Oil is an important ▶ resource found in the Southwest.

▼ Rodeos are popular events in the Southwest.

▲ Millions of years ago, the Colorado River carved out the Grand Canyon.

The West Region

Two states in the West do not border any other state. One is Alaska, the largest state. The other is Hawaii, a group of islands, completely surrounded by water. In this region, you will find the tallest mountains, icebergs, and, of course, movie stars! Fruits and vegetables grow here. Lots of fish and shellfish are caught here, too.

◀ The Rocky Mountains stretch across much of the region. Many people come to the region to ski or snowboard.

Much of the country's fruits and vegetables are grown in the Central Valley in California. ▶

▼ Logging is an important industry in the Pacific Northwest.

▲ California is known for its busy highways. More people live in California than any other state.

15

The United States is made up of 50 states. To find out about each state and the region it is in, turn to the pages listed.

Alabama	8–9	Montana	14–15
Alaska	14–15	Nebraska	10–11
Arizona	12–13	Nevada	14–15
Arkansas	8–9	New Hampshire	6–7
California	14–15	New Jersey	6–7
Colorado	14–15	New Mexico	12–13
Connecticut	6–7	New York	6–7
Delaware	6–7	North Carolina	8–9
Florida	8–9	North Dakota	10–11
Georgia	8–9	Ohio	10–11
Hawaii	14–15	Oklahoma	12–13
Idaho	14–15	Oregon	14–15
Illinois	10–11	Pennsylvania	6–7
Indiana	10–11	Rhode Island	6–7
Iowa	10–11	South Carolina	8–9
Kansas	10–11	South Dakota	10–11
Kentucky	8–9	Tennessee	8–9
Louisiana	8–9	Texas	12–13
Maine	6–7	Utah	14–15
Maryland	6–7	Vermont	6–7
Massachusetts	6–7	Virginia	8–9
Michigan	10–11	Washington	14–15
Minnesota	10–11	West Virginia	8–9
Mississippi	8–9	Wisconsin	10–11
Missouri	10–11	Wyoming	14–15